Social and Political Forces in the English Reformation

THE ROCKWELL LECTURES

The Rice Institute • Houston

Social and Political Forces in the English Reformation

by
CONYERS READ
Emeritus Professor of English History
University of Pennsylvania

HOUSTON
THE ELSEVIER PRESS
1953

SOLE DISTRIBUTORS FOR CONTINENTAL EUROPE:
Elsevier Publishing Company
110 Spuistraat, Amsterdam-C.
FOR THE BRITISH COMMONWEALTH EXCEPT CANADA:
Cleaver-Hume Press, Ltd.
42a South Audley Street, London, W.1.

Library of Congress Catalog Card Number 53-5960

INTRODUCTION

The Rockwell Lectures of the Rice Institute are made possible by the Rockwell Fund, Inc. A series of three lectures annually, the lectures were inaugurated by Sir Robert A. Falconer in April, 1938. Later lectures have been given by Dr. Harris Elliot Kirk, Dean Roscoe Pound, Dr. J. R. Sizoo, Professor William E. Hocking, Dr. Robert R. Wicks, Dr. Ralph W. Sockman, Dr. George A. Buttrick, Professor Charles W. Hendel, Professor Kenneth S. Latourette, Mr. Charles P. Taft, and by Dr. Henry P. Van Dusen.

CONTENTS

I

THE BREAK FROM ROME

There are few subjects in the history of the past on which it is more difficult to reach a definitive judgment than the English Reformation. The principal reason is that the issues of the Reformation are still live issues. A large part of the Christian world still believes that when official England broke from Rome and imposed its decision upon Englishmen, it condemned millions of Englishmen then and since, unless they repented in time, to the eternal bonfire. Probably mankind is less preoccupied about its fate in the world to come than it was in the sixteenth century. But one has only to read the daily papers to realize how deep the issue between Protestant and Roman Catholic still penetrates into our current problems both foreign and domestic.

I remember many years ago when I was a student in London and there was much current agitation in the English press about a proposed public procession of the sacred vessels of the Sacrament from the old to the new Roman Catholic cathedral; my landlady warned me to keep away from the center of the disturbance. If these Papists catch you, she observed, they will burn you at the stake. I do not forget that the good lady probably had Foxe's Book of Martyrs alongside of the family Bible on her parlor table. But her attitude was a not uncommon one. The other side of the story may be read in the

History of the Ku Klux Klan and even in more reputable places.

It is unlikely that the historian himself will altogether escape the influence of these conflicting issues. On that account it becomes a matter of importance, in any appraisal of his position, to inquire whether he is a Protestant or a Catholic. It may even be important to inquire whether the blood in his veins is drawn mainly from English or from Irish or even from Scottish sources. I must begin therefore by confessing that my people on both sides were of English stock, with a tinge, just a tinge, of Irish, – enough, I hope, to provide a sense of humor, but not enough, I fear, to free me from a certain Anglican bias, accentuated no doubt by the unwavering convictions of my devoted Low Church Anglican mother and by two years of residence at an English university. You must make the necessary allowance for these impediments to any dispassionate objectivity.

The historian faces two major problems in his approach to any subject. He must in the first place acquaint himself with the established facts; and he must select, arrange and interpret them in order to discover their significance. It is of course not always easy to decide what facts are really established. Except in contemporary or nearly contemporary history we have no facts at first hand. We have what has been recorded, and we can never be sure that the recorder has been either careful or disinterested. And yet on the whole differences of opinion in history proceed less from a disagreement about the facts than from a disagreement about the significance of them. A large part of our difficulty arises over questions of emphasis. Which is the important, which the unimportant fact and what is their relative importance? The very process of selecting the pertinent facts from all the known facts in itself constitutes a judgment in which all the prejudices and prepossessions of the historian at once come into play. This is notably the case in any complex situation where facts political, economic, social and religious, all contribute their quota. We are well aware that man in all ages has been much concerned about his government, about his bread and butter, about his spiritual welfare. Since we are probably today more politically-minded and more economically-minded than we are spiritually-minded, the temptation always is to emphasize political, and particularly economic considerations, and to discount spiritual considerations. If we are not Marxians, insistent upon economic determinism, we lean too strongly that way in our historical judgments. We know at first-hand the force of the bread and butter question, we are less certain about forces spiritual, and we are on the whole disposed to regard emphasis upon religious considerations as mere hypocrisy. In the sixteenth century, when the service of God was generally regarded as the best of all justifications for action, religion was used as a cover for much that was definitely secular in purpose. Sir Francis Drake, for example, in search of plunder in the South Seas, represented himself as a crusader against "those dogs of Seville, the children of the devil." We are therefore faced with the problem of determining how much that was called religious was in fact religious. Unless we are very careful we shall find ourselves accepting at face value the religious protestations of whose who believe as we do and denouncing as hypocrisy those of opposing creeds. This much I think is certain: that in the sixteenth century the cause of religion was a vital, living reality to a much larger proportion of Christian folk than it is today. No one familiar with the story of the Jesuits in Canada or the pilgrim fathers in Massachusetts can entertain very serious doubts on that point. If we cannot take every sixteenth century crusader at his word we can yet perceive, in his very protestations, the prevalent religious temper of the time. In those days men and women died at the stake for matters in which the great majority of people today have a very languid interest.

In England what we call the Reformation was in its beginnings a political rather than a religious movement; it had to do rather with the government of the church than with its theology. Those indeed who were most active in changing its government were most insistent upon the orthodoxy of their belief. Actually, in its first phase the English quarrel with the Roman Catholic

Church was not that it was Catholic but that it was Roman. We must never forget that the church was not merely the place where one went on Sundays and holy days; it was intimately involved not only in the operations of the government but also in all the details of every-day life. At the top the ecclesiastics were the advisers of kings and formed the majority of the House of Lords. At the bottom the parish was the unit of administrative as well as of religious and social life. The church touched the average Englishmen in all the important crises of his career, at birth through baptism, at adolescence through confirmation, at maturity through marriage, at death through extreme unction. And all along the way, through the confessional and through the pulpit it directed and guided the daily life of the little men. Through its courts it exercised jurisdiction over all clerics, or those who could one way or another establish claim to benefit of clergy. It exercised jurisdiction over all contracts made under oath, over all property bequeathed by will, over all questions of inheritance which turned upon the legitimacy of the offspring involved. If it did not impose capital punishment, it could and indeed did impose ecclesiastical censure which might cut off a man from all the consolations of religion and condemn him to imprisonment until he made his peace with the church. And the law which the church courts administered was not the common law of the land but the canon law, mounting up from court to court not to a supreme court in England but to a supreme court at Rome. In short, the Roman church was a state within a state and the clergy, which included almost all the educated men in England, acknowledged a divided allegiance.

The history of medieval England on the political side is the history of the gradual growth of the power of the crown at the expense of the feudal nobility on the one hand and the ecclesiastical autonomy on the other. It was indeed the history of all the powers in the west. Only in Germany and Italy did the old international concepts of church and state survive. So far as the church was concerned the issues turned upon the jurisdiction of the church courts, the appointment of the upper clergy and the collection of the papal revenues. In England, partly because of the strength of her Norman kings and partly because of her insular position, national strength and national unity were achieved earlier than they were elsewhere. The battle of the crown and the church which began in the twelfth century with Anselm and Becket ebbed and flowed as kings were weak and popes strong and vice versa. Royal power made its great strides forward when the papacy, expelled from Rome, took refuge in South France, lost much of its international character and became in fact the tool of the French crown. This so-called Babylonish captivity of the papacy coincided roughly in time with what we call the Hundred Years War between France and England. As a consequence papal power became identified with French power, that is to say, with the power of the national enemy. It was at this time that the English government enacted those famous statutes of Provisors and Praemunire which had the effect of limiting the papal powers of appointment to church positions in England and of somewhat limiting the right of appeal from English church courts to the supreme court at Rome. Actually these statutes were nothing like so effective in fact as they were on paper. It is always dangerous to assume, for a long time to come, that laws on the statute rolls were consistently enforced. The king always exercised the right to dispense with their operation in particular cases. During the disordered period of the War of the Roses, when the crown was seeking foreign friends wherever they could be found the statutes of Provisors and Praemunire registered what the king might do rather than what he did do. But they reveal the temper of the times in which they were passed and to a marked degree indicate the course which was to be followed in the resumption of the conflict between church and state when, following the War of the Roses, the strong monarchs of the Tudor dynasty reestablished the power of the crown.

The first two Tudors, Henry VII and his son Henry VIII, were both strong men. The father broke what was left of the power of the feudal nobility and the son got rid of the pope. The powers of both these competitors to a strong monarchy passed to the crown. In the actual application of these powers the crown turned to new men, untainted by feudal prestige, selected for their competence and loyalty, altogether dependent upon royal support for their strength, – men like Wolsey and Thomas Cromwell and the Cecils, father and son. If this strengthened the crown it increased the resentment of those of the old feudal aristocracy who still survived, particularly in the peripheral areas north and west. One constant element in almost all the civil disorders in sixteenth century England was hostility to these parvenus. At the local level, the vacuum created by the disruption of local feudal autonomy was filled, not as in France by the establishment of a centralized bureaucracy but by resort to the class just below the nobility, to wit, the country gentry.

In the constitutional history of sixteenth century England probably the most significant development was the increasing importance of the gentry. As justices of the peace they virtually controlled the local administration of justice. As royal officers they dominated practically every department of local administration, the maintenance of roads, the fixing of wages and prices, the direction of poor relief, the levying of troops, the hunting down of religious dissenters. In addition to all this they were the landlords and employers par excellence of the countryside. Before the century was over they had, one way or other, virtually monopolized the seats in the House of Commons. One might almost say that they made the laws as legislators, interpreted the laws as judges and executed the laws as royal officials. Indeed the fact that they controlled the actual application of the laws which they made placed them in the happy position of being able to consult the national interest in the making of laws and their own personal interest in the enforcement of them. As Professor Pickthorne has well said "What the class from which the justices of the peace were drawn wanted done, Tudor monarchs could get done very easily. What they did not mind being done, easily enough. What would happen if the crown should want done some thing which that class was determined should not be done, was a question still to be settled, even still to be raised."[1] Ultimately it was raised with the result that the Tudor pattern of government crashed to the ground.

All of this is important in a consideration of government policy towards religion and towards everything else. Henry VII was himself hardly conscious of the realities of the situation but his son was shrewd enough to perceive that Tudor government was virtually a partnership of king and gentry. While the father, following good medieval precedent, tried his best to get along without parliament, the son took no radical steps in policy without statutory support. He has been well called the greatest parliamentarian who ever sat on the

1. Early Tudor Government. Henry VII, Cambridge, 1934, p. 72.

English throne, the first great royal exponent of government by consent. I do not use the term in the modern democratic sense. Only a small minority of the English in the sixteenth century exercised any political power at all. But if we accept the analysis that power really lay between the king and the gentry, then Henry's great achievement was in drawing the gentry into the picture and imposing upon them a share of the responsibility for his policies. No matter if Henry packed his parliaments or not, no matter if he completely dominated them. What mattered was that he made them an essential feature in his whole scheme of government. At every step in the slow process by which he severed the connection between the church in England and the church in Rome, he had the support of the English parliament behind him.

The immediate occasion of the break from Rome was the desire of the king to get rid of one wife and marry another wife. In order to accomplish that end he could not, under church law, divorce his first wife. He had to demonstrate that his first marriage, being uncanonical, was null and void from the beginning. And he had to get papal approval of that demonstration. Henry had every reason to expect that the pope would lend a favorable ear to his appeal for an annulment of his marriage, – as much had been done both for his brother-in-law and for his sister on far shakier grounds. But Henry's first wife was the aunt of the German emperor,

Charles V, and in the very year in which Henry lodged his appeal the armies of the emperor had occupied Rome and had made the pope virtually a prisoner. So it was that the affair dragged on to interminable length, the pope fearing to alienate Henry by refusing his request, or the all-powerful emperor by granting it. Whatever the merits of the case Henry was in a strong position to main tain that the pope was not a free agent and was not able to give judgment on the merits of the case.

As to the merits of the case, it is certain that Catherine of Aragon, the discarded wife, was a greatly wronged woman and that her brown-eyed rival, Anne Boleyn, was little better than a hussy. But there was more to the matter than a sordid love affair. Catherine had borne Henry many children but only one of them, a daughter, had survived infancy. The Tudor dynasty was still young, its seat on the throne not yet quite firm and the necessity for a male heir great. Nobody at the time took much stock in a female heir, though they were to feel differently about it a generation later when Mary of Lorraine ruled Scotland; Margaret of Parma, the Low Countries; Catherine de Medicis, France; and, greatest of all, Elizabeth, England. Henry who had married his first wife within the prohibited degrees by special dispensation of the pope, began to feel that the lack of a male heir was a definite mark of divine disapproval. Notwithstanding the papal dispensation, the words of Scripture on the subject were plain. "And if a man shall take his brother's wife it is an unclean thing... They shall be childless." This from Leviticus.[1] In Deuteronomy to be sure quite the opposite view was set forth. The fact was that Henry to all effects and purposes was childless. It may be argued, and has been argued, that this was mere hypocrisy on Henry's part, but I think not. He had had his love affairs before and was to have his love affairs again. Indeed he had had a son born out of wedlock ten years before he thought of divorce. But bastards did not solve the problem of the succession. The heir to the throne had to be lawfully begotten. Anne as his mistress might have satisfied the lusts of the flesh, but Henry wanted more than that. Anne knew that he wanted more and declined to accept any position short of marriage. And so it came to pass that, after some seven years of wrangling and the application of steadily increasing pressure by the king, the break came.

Every position which the King took in this running fight was supported in the House of Commons. Why? This raises the fundamental question: Did England at large want to break from Rome?

In the first place it is quite clear that Henry's love affair did not command popular approval. The play of Henry VIII, written long afterwards, in which William Shakespeare had a hand, presents Catherine as the wronged wife and the real heroine of the whole affair.

1. Leviticus, XX, 21.

It probably transmits the traditional popular attitude. Even John Stow, the tailor-historian, writing in the reign of Anne Boleyn's great daughter, paints Catherine in glowing colors and passes over Anne with a bare mention. Henry's case was definitely not strengthened in English eyes by his treatment of his wife.

But what of Rome and the papal supremacy? It must not be forgotten that at this juncture papal supremacy was the one question involved. There could be no doubt at all about Henry's orthodoxy. He had demonstrated it some years before by his attack upon Luther and had won from the pope himself the title Defender of the Faith, which remains to this day a part of the English royal title, though it no longer enjoys papal endorsement. Actually Henry contemplated a reorganization of the western Christian churches by breaking them up into virtually autonomous national units, preserving the unity of the faith with a diversity of government. There were probably relatively few English men with strong, ultra-montaine leanings. They accepted the pope as the symbol of Christian unity, but they were not enthusiastic supporters of his pretensions. Even the English clergy, having tasted the plenitude of papal power when Wolsey was papal legate, were shaken in their loyalty to Rome, so that when the test came they were not too reluctant to exchange papal despotism as Wolsey had imposed it, for royal supremacy. Not the least remarkable feature about Henry's break from Rome was the virtual unanimity with which the English clergy followed his lead. Even among the bishops only one suffered martyrdom for his loyalty to Rome.

It is important to distinguish between loyalty to the pope and loyalty to the faith. In the sixteenth century the one did not necessarily include the other. This was notably true in the case of King Henry himself, and it was equally true of the great majority of his subjects. After the break from Rome, the ritual and the theology of the church in England were models of orthodoxy. The average church-goer, particularly in the remoter parts of England far from the doings of court, was probably unconscious of any change. He still heard the old service in Latin; he still went to confession; he still had his old familiar priest in his old familiar priestly attire, who still baptized his children, married them and performed the last solemn rites at their deathbed. The candles still burned upon the altars, the images of the saints still smiled in stony benignity from their appropriate chapels. The chantry priests still offered their customary masses for the souls of those in purgatory. Such outward and visible signs of the religion in which we have been born and bred are what probably matters to most of us and have probably always mattered. The mysteries of theology are not for us, nor the intricacies of the relations between church and state. The fabric of the church itself, the position of the altar, the colored windows, the pealing organ, the raiment of the priests, the customary prayers, – if you leave them alone, you can go far with church government and even with theology. I wonder how many devout Christians and good church-goers today could explain the official position of their own church upon any one of the questions which have torn the seamless garment of Christ into thousands of discrete fragments. Henry realized this and his great daughter, Elizabeth, was to realize it later. Stephen Gardiner, one of the most learned of Henry's bishops, who fought valiantly for the old forms, expressed the same idea in a letter of protest against proposed innovations which he wrote after Henry's death.

"In the people, for the more number of them, such as be most rude, after a short teaching of God's commandments, they be after led to good life by imitation rather than hearing. They move in the body of the church with much simplicity. And when they have heard words spoken in the pulpit they report they were good, and very good and wondrous good and they were the better to hear them, but what they were they used to profess they cannot tell, unless the manner of it be new and then they marvel and so talk that spake not before. And these we call good men of the country."[1]

But this was not altogether so. Had it been, the Reformation in England might have stopped where Henry's break from Rome had left it. But happily there

1. Letters, Stephen Gardiner, ed. Muller, New York. 1933, p. 311.

were a few who demanded more of religion than the observance of customary rituals and the repetition of customary prayers. Religion for them meant something at once much more simple, much more profound and much more immediate in the relations of a man to his God. They resented the elaborations of ritual and ceremony, the emphasis upon kneeling, upon the symbol, upon the fabric of the church. They resented the intermediation of the priest, particularly if the priest by the impurity of his private life, made mock of his sacred functions. They turned back to the primitive pattern of the primitive church, the pattern as set forth in the New Testament. To them the elaborations of the ecclesiastical structure simply served to obscure and divert the worshipper from things of the spirit to things of the flesh. It has been the fate of all great religions that as their organization has become more complex the outward and visible things have more and more encroached upon the inward and spiritual things. And they have been saved, when they have been saved, from mere ritualism by the protest of earnest believers whose business has been to remind them of their holy purposes. The history of the Roman Church long before the sixtgeenth century is rich with such figures. Church reform did not begin with the Reformation nor did it end with the Reformation. Francis of Assisi, did for the thirteenth century Roman church very much what John Wesley did, or tried to do, for the eighteenth century

Anglican church. Bur Pope Innocent III was wiser than the Anglican church fathers, and Francis was made a saint and John an outcast. The important thing, I think, to remember is that every religious movement tends toward atrophy as it grows older, and provokes impulses for reform.

And yet many of us make the mistake of identifying symbolism with idolatry. It may become idolatry, but its better purpose is to express in concrete terms, particularly to the simple-minded, who in the sixteenth century were by and large illiterate, ideas and ideals which in the abstract lacked warmth and color and even definite meaning. The Christian cross is such a symbol. Our own American flag is such a symbol. Nor can it be denied that there is something in the atmosphere created by ritual and ceremonial which many find congenial for contemplation about the things of the spirtit. The architecture of the church itself sets it off from mere secular buildings. Its association with the more solemn occasions of our lives, baptism, confirmation, marriage, burial, establish it as a place apart. Jesus himself revealed this attitude when he drove the money changers from the temple. One of the greatest of all the Puritans, John Milton, has expressed it in one of his finest passages.

> "But let my due feet never fail,
> To walk the studious cloisters pale.
> And love the high embowèd roof,
> With antique pillars massy proof,

And storied windows richly dight,
Casting a dim, religious light.
Then let the pealing organ blow
To the full-voiced choir below,
In service high and anthems clear
As may, with sweetness, through mine ear
Dissolve me into ecstacies.
And bring all heaven before mine eyes."

Actually these outward and visible things have spiritual value and spiritual significance exactly in proportion to the attitude of the worshipper towards them. I make this point because I think there is too much intolerance among those whose forms of worship are austere towards those who find their religious satisfactions more colorfully.

But symbols can become idols and rituals, vain repetition. And the benefit of clergy can be used to cover the multitude of sins. What the reformers maintained was that the forms and ceremonies had beem emptied of their spiritual content and what they all sought to do was not to destroy but to reform. It was only after they came to dispair of reform that they resorted to open revolt.

In England at any rate, the movement for church reform was a product of that impulse which we call rather vaguely the Renaissance. I am leaving altogether out of account the earlier efforts of John Wyclif and his tattered followers, for there is very little continuity between the Wycliffian movement and the English reform movement of the sixteenth century. Wyclif himself had a profound influence upon the later movement, particularly through the translation of the Bible into English. It was a great achievement, but it came of course before the days of the printing press and its distribution must have been very limited. Actually only two copies of it still survive. Probably there were not many at any time, and in the reaction which followed after Wyclif's death most of them were destroyed. As for his followers, those poor preachers or Lollards as they were contemptuously called, their influence was very limited. But their nickname at least survived and was commonly applied, also contemptuously, to those who came later. One must be careful not to assume, from the continuity of the name, the continuity of the movement.

The sixteenth century impulse came through another channel and found its first striking expression in a small group known as the Oxford Reformers. Of these Sir Thomas More was the outstanding figure, John Colet was another, but the Dutch scholar Erasmus, was the most influential. All of them died in the old faith and both More and Erasmus were its valiant champions in the struggle which followed later with Martin Luther and his theologians. All of them were caustic critics of the scholastic philosophy, all attempted to re-establish the church on the firm foundations of the Bible. "Keep to the Bible and the Apostles Creed," Dean Colet remarked to a group of perplexed theological students, "and let divines if they like dispute about the rest." They believed in the old church, but they rejected with disdain the elaborations of its simple creed by the ingenuity of the Schoolmen, and so they turned to the Bible, intent to find out the truth and confident that an understanding of the truth would give to the old faith new vitality and new significance.

Erasmus himself undertook to produce a more perfect text of the New Testament from the original Greek and published it in 1516. His objective is set forth in his preface. "I utterly dissent", he wrote, "from those who are unwilling that the sacred Scriptures should be read by the unlearned, translated into their vulgar tongue... as though the strength of the Christian religion consisted in men's ignorance of it... I wish that even the weakest woman could read the Gospel... I long that the husbandmen should sing portions of them to himself as he follows the plow, that the weaver should hum them to the tune of his shuttle." John Wyclif himself might have written these words. He would certainly have endorsed them.

The influence of Erasmus was strong at the English universities, particularly strong at Cambridge. By a curious pardox it was strongest in St. John's College, founded a few years before by John Fisher, Bishop of

Rochester, an ardent admirer of Erasmus, equally devoted to the ideas of the reformers and to the old faith. A few years later, Fisher like More was to die a martyr to that faith. Evidently neither of them saw any inconsistency between the new approach to the truth and the established church. At St. John's, a group of scholars arose who rejected the methods of the Schoolmen and directed their efforts toward the study of what they regarded as the authentic sources of Christianity. Since this necessarily involved a study of Greek, they became known as Grecians and the group opposed as Trojans. Among these Grecians were many, like George Day and John Redman and Thomas Watson, who never forsook the old Church, others who were to become the very pillars of the new. The most prominent perhaps were John Cheke and Roger Ascham, and of the same school of thought, scattered among the other Cambridge colleges, Thomas Smith, Matthew Parker, Thomas Cranmer, Hugh Latimer, Nicholas Ridley and William Tyndale. Cheke was to become the close friend and adviser of Edward VI; Ascham the tutor in turn of Edward and his great sister Elizabeth; Smith, Secretary of State under both Edward and Elizabeth; Cranmer, the spiritual head of Henry VIII's national church; Parker the head of Elizabeth's church; Latimer and Ridley, two of the great trilogy of martyrs to the new faith under Catholic Mary; and William Tyndale, who, more than any other single man, made of our English

Bible one of the supremely beautiful literary master-
pieces of our language. These were the men who
really determined the pattern of the English Reformation. It was an academic product in its origin,
springing rather from the classical Renaissance than
from more popular sources. Stephen Gardiner, years
later, was to remark that Erasmus laid the egg which
Luther hatched. Certainly this was true in England and
it was at Cambridge, notably at St. John's College,
Cambridge, that the egg was laid.

I do not intend to suggest that the spirit of reform
was confined to the intellectuals. There were, there probably always had been, in England, individuals and
even little groups of pious simple folk who, failing to
find spiritual satisfaction in the elaborations of the
orthodox ritual, turned to the Bible itself or to such
fragments of the Bible as had been translated into
English. They were not theologians; they were certainly
not rebels. They met in secret and occasionally were
caught and tried as heretics. They were generally la-
beled Lollards. John Foxe, the martyrologist, described
them as the secret multitude of true professors, but
he probably exaggerated, their number.[1] They were
most numerous apparently in the Eastern counties, the
same area which produced later Oliver Cromwell and
his Ironsides. It was an area close to Cambridge on the
one hand and close to the channels of trade with

1. J. M. Parker, the English Reformation to 1558 (Oxford, 1950) p. 19.

Germany on the other. Through those channels the literature of the new German heresy, Lutheranism, began to flow secretly into England. It presently reached Cambridge and fell into the hands of a group of scholars who used to meet, stretch their legs and discuss the sacred mysteries at the White Horse Tavern. It was an informal group, as tavern groups are wont to be, but it included such men as William Paget and Matthew Parker and probably Hugh Latimer and Nicholas Ridley. It may even have included Thomas Cranmer. The most belligerent figures were Robert Barnes and Thomas Bilney, affectionately known as Little Bilney. Bilney and Barnes became active protagonists of unorthodox ideas. Both of them were to suffer martyrdom for the truth as they saw it. The rest of the company were more discreet and when the King, much concerned about his orthodoxy, began a vigorous campaign against Lutheranism, they held their peace. But the seeds were sown in the minds of those scholars who were later to occupy very influential positions in the organization of both the church and state in England.

I do not mean to imply that the English Reformation, even in its initial stages, was Lutheran. Of the great Continental reformers, Martin Luther was the pioneer and his influence was felt first. Later Ulrich Zwingli and John Calvin were to exert their influence, great influence, but as it turned out, peripheral influence. First to last, the English Protestant Reformation was basically English. It borrowed much but always preserved its essentially national character.

There was one other factor of importance in the shaping of English attitudes toward the Roman church – a perennial protest against the worldliness and immorality of the clergymen. This went back at least as far as Langland's Vision of Piers Plowman in the fourteenth century and found eloquent, if somewhat humorous, expression in the writings of Geoffrey Chaucer. It had nothing to do with theology. Certainly neither Langland nor Chaucer had any heretical or rebellious intent, and no doubt Chaucer, at least, exaggerated. Disreputable stories always seemed to gain in point and humor when they are attached to gentlemen of the cloth. But certainly their effect was not to increase reverence for the priesthood. There were besides certain clerical exactions, customary but very distasteful, which stirred up increasing resentment.

There were, for example, the so-called mortuary fees, dues for burial in the consecrated graveyards, which were stretched to include the very shrouds of the dead. They were not heavy but they hit at the wrong time, sometimes at the very grave of the departed. They hit at the wrong time when Richard Hunne, a prosperous London merchant, stood by and watched a predatory priest snatch the winding sheet from the body of his dead baby. Hunne, enraged, brought suit to recover. He lost his suit, carried the matter further, was charged with heresy, imprisoned and ultimately found hanged in his cell. The church said suicide, a London coroner's jury said murder. The matter did not end there. It was carried to the House of Commons and led to a long dispute over the liberties of the clergy in which the King himself had to intervene. It came before the House of Commons again in 1529, the Commons of that reformation parliament which was to sit for six years and to legalize every step in the break from Rome. The first measure introduced in that famous body was a bill to correct the evils of mortuary dues for which Hunne had suffered. It was, as Mr. Ogle has observed[1], the opening stroke in something like a vendetta which reached its bitterest in the supplication of the commons against the bishops of 1532 and made straight the way for the ultimate break with Rome.

The treatment of Hunne should not be taken as typical of the behavior of the old English clergy. It does, however, supply perhaps the best illustration of an attitude of developing antipathy on the part of the English Commons towards the clergy which was an important factor in securing parliamentary endorsement of the King's break from Rome.

That break was practically complete by 1535. It was followed almost at once by a royal attack upon the property of the old church which constitutes the most unsavory part of the story. I refer of course to the

1. The Tragedy of the Lollard's Tower (Oxford, 1949), p. 366.

dissolution of the English monasteries. When all has been said that can be said about the shortcomings of the English monastic establishments the grim fact still remains that they were systematically plundered not because of their shortcomings but because of their wealth. Leaving out of account the treasures of the shrines and the church plate, the annual rental value of the monastic lands was more than double the annual expense of the government at the end of Henry's reign.[1] It represented a very considerable part of the landed wealth of England. In the last decade of Henry's reign when two-thirds of this land was sold or given away, the sale yielded nearly £ 800,000. The remaining third constituted an important reserve which may have played a decisive part in saving England from the national bankruptcy which descended upon both France and Spain later in the century. The whole transaction indubitably solved Henry's financial problems. What was more important it more or less committed all those who had secured any part of these lands, either by gift or purchase, to the support of Henry's religious policy. Among these the most considerable beneficiaries were Edward Seymour and John Dudley, the two men who were to rule England after Henry's death. Virtually every prominent courtier and royal servant had a finger in the pie. The mercantile classes were deeply engaged

1. H. A. L. Fisher, *Political History of England, 1485–1547*, pp. 497–98.

and there were many instances of Londoners clubbing together to make joint purchases. A good many of those who bought, bought on speculation, to sell again. In short, the nobles, the gentry and the prosperous town-folk all had good money in monastic property.[1] This fact probably presented the most considerable obstacle to a whole-hearted return to Roman Catholicism under Henry's Catholic daughter. The economic and social consequences of the wholesale transfer of land from old owners to new owners were even more far-reaching.

Certainly Henry VIII when he broke from Rome did not foresee the religious and economic consequences which were to follow. He wanted to keep the church as it was, only under another head; he wanted to keep old England as it was. But even he, strong man though he was, turned out to be the blind agent of forces which were much stronger than he.

1. Liljegren, the Fall of the Monasteries (Lund, 1924), pp. 109 ff.

II

THE ANGLICAN ESTABLISHMENT

When Henry VIII broke from Rome he never intended to break from the old faith. But the situation in contemporary Europe more or less forced his hand. On the one side the movement for church reform was steadily growing. In 1535 Lutheranism had already established itself strongly in Germany. Another reform movement was spreading rapidly in Switzerland. In France John Calvin was in the very act of publishing his Institutes, perhaps the most important single book, outside the Bible itself, in the whole history of the Reformation. On the other side, the Roman Church, awake at last to the menace which threatened its integrity, was girding itself for battle. In 1534 Ignatius Loyola had founded the Jesuit Order, which was presently to become the chief instrument in the battle of the old order against the new. And in the same year came a new pope, Paul III, who, whatever his shortcomings, was aware of the seriousness of the situation and began to organize the resources of the old church in its defense.

One might almost say that the year which marked Henry's break from Rome marked also the emergence of the Roman Catholic Counter Reformation as an effective fighting force. Thenceforward western Christendom increasingly aligned itself into two camps, and old dynastic rivalries, which had dominated international relations during the first third of the sixteenth century, began to yield place to the rivalries of the contending creeds. Yet this was never altogether so. Neither the leaders of the Reformation nor the leaders of the Counter Reformation were ever quite able to consolidate their strength behind their objective.

The Protestant ranks were gravely weakened by disagreement over dogma, over ritual and over that thorny question of the relations of church and state. On the Catholic side the cause of the international church had to contend with the rising nationalism within the several Catholic states. Rivalry between France and Spain, between France and the Empire, between Hapsburg and Valois, in the long run prevented any effective realization of a united crusade of the faithful against the heretics.

Yet even so, the increasing emphasis upon religious issues brought a new element into the situation which even an ardent nationalist like Henry VIII could not altogether ignore. His break from Rome more or less implied, though he resented the implication, his break with Charles V who was at once Emperor of the German nation, King of Spain and of the fabulously wealthy dominions of Spain in the New World, Duke of Burgundy, Master of a large part of Italy; and with Francis I, King of France. Henry did not altogether despair of being able to play the one against the other. But he was forced, against his will, to establish relations

{ 29 }

and strengthen connections with the fighting forces of Protestantism in Germany. This necessarily involved some effort to find a common platform on religious issues. Henry opened negotiations with the German Protestants as early as 1534, and they dragged on intermittently until 1540. In the end they accomplished nothing, but in their course some approximation to the German position was attempted in England. Thomas Cranmer, Archbishop of Canterbury, and the closest of Henry's ecclesiastical advisers, was hopeful and the earliest of his surviving projects for liturgical reform, dating probably from 1537, bore a strong resemblance to Luther's Kirchenordnungen. The Ten Articles, which in 1536 embodied the royal declaration of faith, revealed a marked German influence and the long exchange of ideas between German and English theologians did bear fruit after Henry's death.

But Henry's purposes were political rather than religious. He never cherished what was one of Cranmer's dreams, the idea of Protestant unity. As his fears of a combination of the Roman Catholic powers against him waned, his enthusiasm for an effective alliance with the Lutherans waned also. The last straw was the fiasco of the marriage with Anne of Cleves – the Flemish mare as Henry called her. Thomas Cromwell, who had engineered the match, was sent to the block, and Henry re-asserted his complete orthodoxy in the famous Six Articles established by act of Parliament. Thereafter for a season the conservatives dominated the old King's religious program. But they in turn lost pre-eminence as the royal marriage with Catherine Howard, which had marked their establishment in the royal favor, was blasted by the infidelity of that frail and lovely lady. Henry's last wife, Catherine Parr, was a secret friend of reform, and she probably exercised an influence in that direction upon her royal spouse during the last years of his life. Certainly when he established a regency to manage the affairs of the kingdom during the minority of his young son, he definitely rejected Stephen Gardiner, the leader of the conservatives, and placed the reins of power in the hands of the other party.

But there are very few other indications of any strong interest on Henry's part in the program of the reformers. Up until the moment of his death the Six Articles expressed the official faith and they did not differ in any essential particular, except of course the papal supremacy, from the orthodox Roman Catholic position.

The one exception was the official endorsement of an English translation of the Bible. Shortly after Henry had issued the Ten Articles in 1536 a series of injunctions went out to the clergy, directing them to teach children the Lord's Prayer, the Creed and the Ten Commandments in English. Within the year a Bible in Latin and in English was to be placed in the choir of every parish church for everyone to read. This evidently did not refer to the one extant printed version of the Bible, William Tyndale's version, which was a proscribed book and six years before had been publicly burned in St. Paul's Churchyard. In fact there was no authorized English version of the Bible available. Two years later one was provided. It was printed by the royal printer and dedicated to the King by one who signed himself Thomas Matthew, probably a pseudonym for John Rogers, later burned at the stake in Mary's reign. By a singular act of retribution, all of the New Testament in the official Bible was directly derived and largely copied from the version of William Tyndale, who had been hunted to his death for the making of it some twelve years before. Henry subsequently undertook to limit the reading of the Bible to the gentry, but by that time it had spread far and wide. And what Erasmus had prayed for and Tyndale had promised had come to pass. And the plowman at his plow and the weaver at his loom drank deep of the Gospel at the well-springs. Nothing which Henry VIII did, perhaps nothing which was ever done, played so large a part in the triumph of the Reformation in England. The New Testament as we read it today, in the magnificent English of the authorized version, is mainly Tyndale's work. He did it in exile, a hunted man. When he was caught at last and tied to the stake to suffer for what he had done, he lifted up his head and prayed "Lord, open the King of England's eyes." In a strange oblique sort of way, his prayer was answered. Henry probably never knew, but we know. And in the light of that knowledge we must never forget that though there was much that was mere power politics, much that was mere greed, in the break from Rome, there was also William Tyndale who read in the Gospel story the promise of a richer, more significant and more abundant life and who gave the last full measure of his devotion to the business of revealing that promise to his fellows.

When Henry died he left the crown to a child, the government to a group of councillors who had long served him in positions of trust. The outstanding figures were Thomas Cranmer, Archbishop of Canterbury; Edward Seymour, Earl of Hertford, the young king's uncle; William Paget, the old king's trusted secretary, and John Dudley, Earl of Warwick. All of these men belonged to the left wing of the old King's council, all of them endorsed and approved the break from Rome. Paget and Warwick were primarily politicians, more interested in problems of power than problems of faith. Warwick, at his death, professed himself to be a loyal Roman Catholic, though little in his life revealed that fact. Paget was to become secretary under Mary the Catholic. But Seymour probably, and Cranmer certainly, meant to carry the Reformation considerably beyond the position of Henrican Catholicism.

Among those below the top level in government the reformers were strong. There were, for example, John

Cheke, Thomas Smith and young William Cecil, Elizabeth's great minister, who was just entering public life. Smith was presently to become one of the principal secretaries, and a little later Cecil, and a little later still, Cheke. These lesser men were not making policy, but they were in a very favorable position to influence the policy-makers. They were all Cambridge University men, all Grecians, one or two of them probably out of the White Horse Tavern group. We have here something like a brain trust. Indeed the whole Reformation movement during Edward's reign was engineered by a small group of men, classical scholars for the most part, who were in sympathy with many of the basic ideas of the Lutheran reformers but were to move to the left cautiously and gradually. There were very few zealots among them, and no martyrs.

As to the people at large, probably the power-possessing classes, the gentry and the new nobility, like the Seymours and the Dudleys and the Russells and the Herberts and the Parrs, definitely endorsed the break with Rome if for no other reason than because they had large property interests at stake. It is not easy to appraise the religious attitudes of the great mass of the people. They were probably not dissatisfied with the Henrican arrangements, since Henry had made very few changes in the old ritual or in the old personnel of the church. To the average Englishman, not much concerned with the higher reaches of church government, the church appeared to be what the church had always been. There was a considerable sentiment in favor of reform in London and in the eastern counties. But they were not representative. The rest of England was not interested in change. In the north and west, the sentiment was strong that change had gone too far already.

The reform party at court cherished no illusions on the subject. They were sure they were right but they did not undertake to impose their pattern by force. Seymour, now become Duke of Somerset and Lord Protector, was a broad-minded, liberal man in his thinking, one of the first of the English latitudinarians. So was Cranmer. All they tried to do during their first year in power was to remove old restraints. They tacitly ignored the laws against heresy and virtually threw open the pulpit to preachers of all complexions. There sult was widespread disorder, some image-breaking in London and elsewhere, and a veritable whirlwind of scurrilous ballads and tracts against the Catholic mass. Actually the government, in the interests of peace, was more concerned with restraining the zeal of the agitators than in supporting them. When Parliament met at the end of the year it did little more than repeal the old heresy laws and the Six Articles and remove all legal restraints upon the reading, the teaching and the expounding of the Scriptures. It did establish the celebration of the Communion service in both kinds, that is to say, it authorized the giving of both the wine and the bread to the communicants, an innovation which ran counter to the common practice in the Catholic Church. But it is to be noted that this law was passed at the request of the clergy themselves and that those who followed the new rite were strictly enjoined not to condemn those outside the kingdom who adhered to the old one.

The one drastic act had to do with a further wholesale plunder of church property by abolishing the chantries and confiscating their endowments. These chantries had been established for the purpose of saying prayers for the souls of the dead in Purgatory. The abolition of them implied a rejection of the whole doctrine of Purgatory. But this was no novelty. Even the orthodox Henry VIII had taken definite steps in the same direction. The intention was expressed of devoting the confiscated property to the establishment of grammar schools, but actually the great bulk of it went the same way as the monastic lands, into the pockets of the gentry.

During most of the year following, government action with reference to matters religious generally took the form of preventing sacrilege, unlicensed preaching and deviation from the established procedures in religious observance. The necessity of a greater degree of uniformity was recognized, and the indications are that Somerset and Cranmer were casting about to find a formula which would satisfy their own convictions and at the same time be generally acceptable to the people.

An important factor in Cranmer's thinking was the disasters which had been falling upon the Protestant causes in Germany, beginning with the defeat at Muhlenberg in the spring of 1547 and finding expression in the so-called Interim of 1548. The effect of all this was a considerable migration of German Protestants to England, most of whom came in response to Cranmer's personal invitation. It was at this juncture that the ideas of the Continental reformers exercised probably their greatest influence upon the development of the Anglican creed. Cranmer indeed cherished the hope that a way might be found to draw all the Protestant churches into one fold. The refugees who came represented many variations of opinion, the main point at issue among them being the significance of the Mass, or, in Protestant terminology, of the Holy Communion, the Lord's Supper. Luther and Zwingli had broken sharply on the subject. Luther insisted upon the corporeal presence of the body and blood of Christ in the bread and wine of the Communion. Zwingli maintained that there was no such mystical transformation, that the bread and the wine were simply precious symbols of Christ's sacrifice for men and not in themselves of His essence. Actually, there were no orthodox Lutherans among the refugees. The most influential of them seemed to have taken an intermediate position. It was this position which Cranmer himself favored. He accepted the miracle of the Mass but maintained that it resided not in any corporeal change in the elements but in a spiritual change in the communicants. The mouth received the bread and wine, the worthy soul fed upon the very body and blood of Christ. The miracle was, in short, contingent upon the faith of the communicant. Without that the bread and the wine lost their sacramental character.

The important difference from the orthodox Roman position was that the miracle was effected by the faith of the communicant, not by the intercession of the priest. There was "no making of God", as Wycliff put it, by clerical ritual. At the same time much of the old ceremonial could be preserved. Actually this position became the orthodox position of the Anglican Church and is set forth today in the 39 Articles of the Anglican faith. But the orthodox Lutherans would have none of it and the Zwinglians would have none of it. So it never served to advance Cranmer's hopes of Protestant unity. On the suface it appears like a compromise. And superficially it was. But we need not assume that Cranmer was a mere trimmer, any more than we need assume that any position midway between extremes reflects a sacrifice of ideals to expediency. Cranmer's primary purpose was to establish a church which would preserve as much of the traditional pattern of worship as was not inconsistent with the basic principles of the reformers. He was far from being an iconoclast, far from being doctrinaire. Like all the reformers, he drew his ideas from the Bible. But he recognized that the Bible was not the only channel through which God had revealed himself and he found much in the old faith to cherish and perpetuate. The English prayer-book, as he designed it, was in very large measure a translation of Latin prayers out of the old service books. I think he regarded much about which the theologians wrangled as matters of secondary importance. But like everyone else in the sixteenth century he insisted upon uniformity of worship. Men then no more thought of the possibility of many faiths and mutual tolerance than they thought of many states within the state. Cranmer would have maintained, as Richard Hooker was to maintain later, that the church was made up of the same people as made up the nation, – was simply the state at its devotions. He was in short a good Erastian, a convinced believer in the royal supremacy. But he was also a good liberal, and under the king he wanted the church to be as broad and comprehensive as it might be. Somerset was of the same way of thinking and as long as Somerset and Cranmer worked together that was their program of reform. They clearly did not wish to impose their ideas by force. That probably explains why they threw open the pulpit and the press. They cherished that fond hope which we all cherish – that by free and open discussion men would at last discern the truth and follow it.

After a year of profitless wrangling, in high places

and low, with every variety of religious observance in the churches, it became apparent, if only in the interests of public order, that some official pattern should be defined and imposed. That was the genesis of the first Book of Common Prayer. It was mainly the work of Cranmer himself, who laid his draft before a commission, made up chiefly of bishops of the church, in September, 1548. We have no record of any discussion. Only one of the bishops refused to accept the book, though many of them were not prepared to endorse it in all particulars. It was laid before the Parliament, which met later in the autumn, for approval. There was considerable opposition to it in the House of Lords though in the final vote only three temporal peers voted against it, and the majority of the bishops supported it. There is very little evidence of any opposition to it in the Commons. It passed late in January, 1549.

The decision of Parliament was expressed in an Act of Uniformity which established the Prayer-book and prohibited all other forms of worship in England. But its penalties fell solely upon those clergymen who administered other forms of service. There was no compulsion imposed upon the worshipper to attend the church, no penalties for non-attendance, no attempt of censure personal and private beliefs. The purpose of the act was expressed in the mildest terms. It recalled the various forms of service commonly used in England before the break from Rome and stated its intention to bring them all together into a common form. There was no attack upon the old church, no denunciation of the papacy, no attempt to identify the English church with the Continental Reformation. Certainly it was the mildest act of uniformity ever imposed. Even the Prayer-book, except in the Communion service, did not deviate far from the old ritual or the old vestments. Had it not been in English instead of Latin the average churchgoer could hardly have perceived the difference. And what it lost to those accustomed to the old language it more than regained in the singular beauty of its superb English. It is not a book of theology, it is a book of devotion. As an expression of the essentials of the Christian faith, irrespective of denominations, it remains to this day the supreme example. It was mainly the work of Thomas Cranmer and nothing that he did, probably nothing that anyone else has done, has been so potent in establishing the claims of the Church of England upon the loyalty of its supporters. The rhythmic cadences of its beautiful prayers sing themselves today in the devotions of thousands of Christians outside the Anglican communion.

The years 1548 and 1549 were years of troubles, troubles economic and social as well as religious. The root of all these troubles was the rise of prices. It was at this point that the new world upset the balance of the old. The result of the Spanish conquest of Mexico and Peru was to pour into the European money market large quantities of gold and silver. It had exactly the same effect that any sudden expansion of the amount of money in circulation has. It shot prices up. Actually in the course of the sixteenth century prices multiplied three-fold and the cost of living increased accordingly. Unfortunately, as many of us since have discovered to our sorrow, incomes did not increase proportionately. This was particularly true of those types of income which were relatively inflexible, like professors' salaries and land rentals. The land-owning classes in England, by and large the nobility and the gentry, presently discovered that rents fixed by custom could not be increased at will. If this was true of the land they rented out, it was no less true of the land they farmed themselves. The old agricultural economy, though it sustained the agricultural population, yielded comparatively little in the way of surplus which could be converted into cash. How then were the landowners to keep abreast of the increased cost of living? They might raise their rents – and they did where they could. Rack renting, so-called, was one of the crying grievances of the century. Or they might abandon the old methods of tillage, which in the absence of adequate fertilization, was yielding a steadily diminishing return.

The obvious answer was to turn from tillage to grazing. There was a steady market in Europe for English wool, currently regarded as the finest in the world. By converting from arable land to pasture the landowner could produce a much more profitable crop at a much lower overhead expense. It was indubitably good business but it had very damaging social consequences. As one reformer bitterly remarked, "Where sixty persons had their livings, now one man and his shepherds hath all." What we have here really are the birth throes of the capitalistic economy in English agriculture. Its immediate result was the wholesale eviction of small people from their lands and the transformation of the small independent cultivator into an agricultural wage-earning laborer. Tudor governments tried their best to stem this movement. Contrary to the general impression they were in the main conservative in their economic policy and their efforts were pretty consistently directed towards the preservation and defense of the customary arrangements. This was largely due to the widespread popular discontent engendered by the change and the great increase in unemployment. As religion was one important factor involved in the domestic uprisings of the sixteenth century, protest against the new economy was another. What the Tudors wanted was stability.

The country gentry were of another mind. They were prepared to support Somerset's religious policy so long as it did not effect their self-interest. They were prepared to enact laws against the new economy in Parliament, so long as they could control the application of these laws in fact. Somerset himself believed that the law should be enforced, and there was a group of men around him who were of the same mind, men like Hugh Latimer and John Hales – Commonwealth Men, they were called, – and they spread their views from the pulpit and in the press. They were not democrats; they were staunch adherents to that social pattern which Professor Lovejoy has called The Great Chain of Being, a pattern which assigned to every man, not an equal place, but a divinely appointed place in God's scheme of things. Every such place had its rights, every place its responsibilities. Upon the governing class God had imposed the obligation of protecting and maintaining the common welfare. "The Commons and poor people be members of that body that nobles and rich men be. And surely such as desire the king's honor and safety and the wealth and surety of the realm will direct all their study to increase and maintain all the king's majesty's subjects generally, every one in his degree, and not go about to diminish and weaken them." So John Hales wrote[1]. Like almost all the social reformers of the sixteenth century, he blamed the social evils of the time on those who were charged with the business of government. His answer was either moral regeneration or vigorous law enforcement. Some time before Sir Thomas More had made his own observations upon the exploitation of power by the governing class in their own interest:

1. A Discourse of the Commonweal (ed. Lamond, Combridge, 1893), p. lx.

"When I consider and weigh in my mind", he wrote, "all these Commonwealths which now-a-days any where do flourish, so God help me, I can perceive nothing but a certain conspiracy of rich men, procuring their own commodities under the name and title of the Commonwealth."

More, in despair, turned from practical politics to escape in Utopia – the land of nowhere. But Somerset and Hales, men of action, meant to do things about it. If the gentry placed particular wealth before Commonwealth then the gentry must be dealt with. Somerset's first idea apparently was the old device of passing new laws. When Parliament failed to support him in that course, he resorted to the same techniques which Wolsey had applied earlier, the technique of sending royal commissioners into the counties to enforce compliance. When he proposed this course to the King's council they were unanimously opposed. But he went ahead nevertheless "Maughere the devil, private profit, self-love, money, and such like the devil's instruments" he said to Hales, "it shall go forward."[1]

But he reckoned without his host. All that his efforts really accomplished was to give a certain endorsement to local uprisings against enclosures and to antagonize those upon whom he had to depend for support. The vigor with which Somerset pushed his social reforms was to be his undoing. He was branded a libertarian, his

1. Tytler, England under Edward VI and Mary (London, 1839) i, 116.

followers were denounced as Anabaptists – the sixteenth century equivalent of Communists. The gentry accepted his religious policy because they had interests at stake. They resisted his economic policy because there also they had interests at stake. As for his concern with the welfare of the common man, they saw in it simply a stimulus to disorder. In some parts of England the opposition to enclosures was part of a larger opposition against novelties in government and novelties in religion. In other parts it went hand-in-hand, as it did in Norfolk, with zeal for the new faith. The common folk called Somerset the Good Duke. In a democratic society that would have been a great asset, but in the society of that day, it was a liability. The property classes wanted, above everything else, public order. That was why religious reformers made so much of obedience to constituted authority. They were always afraid that the changes they worked for in the church would be coupled in the English mind with an attack upon property, the kind of attack revealed in the Peasants' Revolt in Germany, and more immediately in Ket's revolt in Norfolk. So even the reformers looked upon Somerset's economic policy askance.

The consequence was that those who opposed Somerset in the council overthrew him. The leader of that opposition was John Dudley, Earl of Warwick, later to be Duke of Northumberland, a politician par excellence. The opposition he organized was a kind of

Cave of Adullam, a gathering-together of all those who for any reason were discontented with Somerset's government. The gentry were promised that they would be left alone in their agricultural changes, the Roman Catholics were deluded by the hope of a religious reaction in their favor. And so Somerset, charged with all sorts of fantastic conspiracies, was seized and thrown into the Tower. He got off with what was for the times a very light punishment, but he ceased to be Lord Protector and the effective leadership of the government passed to Warwick.

It is customary to assume that Warwick intended the destruction of Somerset from the first. But I am not so sure. Certainly the relations between the two during the six months following Somerset's fall from power were friendly in the extreme, friendly even to the point that Somerset's daughter married Warwick's oldest son. There can be no doubt that Somerset's economic program was definitely abandoned. Parliament saw to that. The thirteenth century statute of Merton which had authorized enclosure was re-enacted and heavy punishments were imposed upon political and social agitators.

In matters religious Warwick had held out hope of large concessions to the Roman Catholics, but he abandoned any pretense in that matter as soon as he was securely in the saddle. Actually he went much further to the left in matters religious than Somerset had ever been prepared to go. Since Warwick was a man without religious convictions his decision to support the more radical reformers may be taken to indicate that he regarded them as the winning side. The readiness with the House of Commons accepted his program of religious reform gave him some warrant for his belief. But the House of Commons spoke for the gentry. There is very little evidence of enthusiasm among the people at large. Warwick foresaw that the young king had not long to live and that it was very important for the beneficiaries of the break from Rome to strengthen their position before the succession passed to the heir presumptive, Mary, the resolute champion of the old faith. It was reasonably certain that if Mary did succeed she would undertake to re-establish the old faith. And that would probably involve not only the return to Rome but the restitution of church property.

Even convinced reformers like young William Cecil regarded the prospect as a grim one. In a memorandum on the subject a year after Somerset's fall he wrote, "We are not agreed among ourselves. The majority of our people will support the adversary. So long as all is quiet the king can preserve the peace but should war break out the people will listen rather to what they will consider the voice of God, calling on them to restore the papacy, than to the voice of the king calling on them to obey. The great body of the peers, some of the council, all the bishops except three or four, almost all the judges and lawyers, almost all the justices of the peace, the priests and vicars will be on the same side. And the commons are in such a state of irritation that they will rise at a word."[1]

Cecil was pleading for peace, but what he wrote in November 1550 foreshadowed what came to pass when the young king died less than three years later. What Warwick wanted was the continuance of his own power and his own wealth and that was what his supporters wanted. Sir Thomas More's description fitted them exactly – "A conspiracy of rich men seeking their own commodity under the name of the Commonwealth." They were not concerned with the popular wish, not nearly enough with the popular support. They were in no sense seeking a solution of the religious problem on its merits. They wanted to close the door to any accommodation between the old and the new, and they wanted to lay their hands on more ecclesiastical property. If they could justify plunder of the shrines and the sacred vessels by labeling them idolatrous, so much the better. The program of the radical reformers was therefore much better adapted to their purposes than that of the moderates. It is a sad picture. Naturally, the radicals regarded Warwick as their champion and described him in their correspondence as "the intrepid soldier of Christ". Had they had their way they would have cleared away the last vestiges of the old faith, the ritual, the

1. Froude, History of England (ed. Scribner, 1899) v. 285.

vestments, the altar, the cross. Almost all of them looked for inspiration to Henry Bullinger, Zwingli's successor as leader of the Swiss reformers at Zurich, or to John Calvin at Geneva.

Cranmer, still head of the English church, resisted them as much as he dared. Somerset began to explore the possibility of a compromise with the Catholics. Undoubtedly he did take some steps in the direction of a conspiracy to depose Warwick, but he was a bad conspirator and he grossly exaggerated his political strength. Even his old supporters like William Cecil had attached themselves to Warwick's regime, and he had almost no friends left in high places. The fact is that the political realists in England of all complexions regarded the situation as so precarious that they dared not run the risk of a civil war. They probably agreed that Somerset was the better man of the two, as indeed he was, but his return to power promised little more than an increase of civil disorders and perhaps even a definite alignment of the masses against the classes which everybody who mattered regarded as the worst thing that could happen. Somerset was devoted to the cause of religious reform and is entitled to share with Cranmer the distinction of having defined the Church of England as in all essential features it was to be. And he had an interest in the welfare of the common man which few of his class shared. But he loved power and he loved riches, and towards the end he fell more and more under the spell of a small irresponsible group who in pursuit of their own interests drove him forward, against the whole current of the times, to his inevitable destruction. One factor probably was his masterful and ambitious wife. Undoubtely his attentions were good, but they were distorted by personal ambitions. Certainly he was not wise in his generation. His position in matters religious and indeed in matters economic anticipated those of Queen Elizabeth, but he lacked her power and he lacked her instinctive sense of the realities of the situation – her acceptance of the frame of reference in which her power could alone be successfully applied. He ignored the basic principle which underlay the whole Tudor concept of government – that it was fundamentally a partnership of the crown and the gentry.

Somerset had an edifying end and passed into popular legend as the Good Duke. His execution added considerably to the mounting total of Warwick's unpopularity. After his death the right wing reformers had to yield still further to the left-wing reformers. John Hooper, later known as the Father of Non-Conformity, became Warwick's particular protégé. At one time he even proposed John Knox for the bishopric of Rochester, but later changed his mind as that doughty Scotchman revealed himself as "neither grateful nor pleaseable." Both Hooper and Knox shared the position of the Swiss reformers on the thorny question of the

Lord's Supper. And both of them wanted to go much further than Cranmer was prepared to go in what they would have called "cleansing the English Church of its Popish attributes." They accomplished something but on the whole not very much.

The second Book of Common Prayer issued in 1552 gives some measure of their influence. As compared with the first Prayer-book the most striking change was made in the celebration of communion. According to the first Prayer-book the minister was to say, as he offered the bread to the communicants, "The body of our Lord Jesus Christ which was given for thee preserve thy body into everlasting life." And so with the wine. In the second Prayer-book he was to say "Take, eat this in remembrance that Christ died for thee and feed on him in they heart by faith with thanksgiving." The altar is still an altar in the first Prayer-book, it has become a table in the Second. The customary vestments provided in the first are omitted in the second. And though in both the communicants are still to receive the bread and the wine on their knees, a footnote, the famous Black Rubric, in the second book explained that the act of kneeling implied no adoration of the elements.

The second Prayer-book like the first was imposed by Parliament in a second Act of Uniformity, which like the first forbade the use of all other services in England. Unlike the first, it not only imposed penalties upon those who administered any other form of service but it also imposed penalties upon the laity for non-attendance at the established church. What the law now said was that there should be only one service in England and that every Englishman should attend that service, or else. It marked a definite tightening of the screws, the first serious attempt to impose the new religion by force. Its history was too brief to supply any adequate evidence of its effectiveness, but it did define the policy which was to be followed by the government in dealing with religious dissent for over a century to follow.

In the last few months of Edward's reign the king published an official statement of the English official creed in the so-called Articles of the Faith – the Forty-two Articles. They had been drafted by Cranmer and they reflected his position in the matters in controversy. With no significant changes they were subsequently, under Elizabeth, incorporated in the Thirty-nine Articles which remain to this day the basic formula of the Anglican church.

In fact, therefore, the Anglican establishment, in all its essential particulars, was clearly defined in the reign of Edward VI. The liturgy as set forth in the second Book of Common Prayer was modified in one essential particular. The words to be spoken by the minister in the administration of the communion, as set forth in the first book of Common Prayer, were in the Elizabethan prayer-book added to those as set forth in the Second

Edwardian book. In short, the Elizabethan liturgy was somewhat more conservative than Edward's second book, somewhat more radical than his first book. But in general the good Anglican today, reading Edward's second book, would find it entirely familiar, though he would miss some of the prayers, notably the exquisitely beautiful General Thanksgiving, which was contributed later. So the liturgy, the articles of faith, the church government and the policy of imposing uniformity, blended together in Edward VI's reign, defined in all its essential points the Anglican establishment. All that Elizabeth and her theologians did later was to modify it a little here and there, to explain it and to justify it. She did not create it. Henry VIII laid the foundation by establishing the royal headship, but it was Thomas Cranmer who informed it with a new spirit and illuminated it with a rare beauty. He was the architect of the Anglican establishment, and though he was a frail man, who made many compromises with smaller differences in the interests of a larger unity, in the end he died a martyr to vindicate his handiwork.

The surprising thing about John Dudley, Earl of Warwick, and Duke of Northumberland, unchallenged master of England, was his fall. He controlled the machinery of government, commanded the support of all the big men, and dominated the young king even to the point of inducing him to alter the course of the succession in favor of Dudley's daughter-in-law, the unfortunate Lady Jane Grey, and yet he fell. England would have none of him. As soon as the young king died, as soon as Mary the Catholic had raised her standards, the English almost to a man rallied to her support. It is easy to explain Warwick's unpopularity, but not so easy to explain why his henchmen, who had built up their fortunes from the spoils of the old church, turned to a woman who stood above all things else for the old church. Certainly it was not zeal for the old church, though obviously there was not enough zeal for the new church to prevent it. The new church indeed suffered not a little contamination from its association with Dudley's regime. It was not any magnetism in Mary's own personality, though Mary had her great moments. At bottom it was perhaps a national revulsion of feeling against gangster rule and the tossing about of the royal crown by an adventurer. National pride was involved, national self-respect and that deep reverence for what we may broadly call legitimacy, which is one of the basic characteristics of the English breed.

Mary came to the throne on a wave of national enthusiasm. But it did not last long. She was half-Spanish in blood, and though she had many English attributes it was the Spanish half of her which directed her purposes. Her dominating interests were her Spanish husband and her Roman faith. It was this pre-occupation with interests not English which was her undoing.

The developing opposition to her was clearly not religious. Had she been content with a return to the Henrican Catholicism of her father, she would probably have come closer to the religious views of the great masses of her subjects than her brother ever did. Had she married an Englishman, she would have satisfied the universal demand that she should marry and have satisfied also the well-nigh universal demand that her marriage should not involve England in continental broils. Nobody, not even Elizabeth's most loyal supporters, contemplated with equinimity a virgin queen, and there were few Englishmen who were not fundamentally isolationist in their international attitudes. Mary made an important contribution to the progress of the Reformation in England by establishing a close association in the English mind between the old faith and the Spanish connection. Her persecution of the heretics, though it was mild enough as compared with what was happening in other Catholic countries, was unique in England. Even to Englishmen who were opposed to religious reform it looked like a barbarian display of Spanish influence. It might be good doctrine but it was not British. And so the Protestant martyrs became in a sort of way martyrs not only to their faith but to their Englishry.

What Englishmen saw in Mary's whole policy was the complete subordination of English interests and English ways of doing things to a foreign pattern.

Catholicism, yes, but Rome, no. Marriage, yes, but a foreign Spanish marriage, no. Religious uniformity, yes, but not by the auto-da-fé and the stake. What Mary did was to identify the old church with Spain and the Protestant cause with the national interest. Her treatment of the heretics, though most of them were little men or clerics – not a single gentleman died for his faith – produced such abundant evidence of gallant devotion that it did more to arouse interest in reform than to check it. Londoners of all faiths were both sickened and inspired by the fires of Smithfield and all England rang with those magnificent cheering words of Hugh Latimer as he stood side by side with Nicholas Ridley at the stake at Oxford. "Be of good cheer, Master Ridley. We shall this day light such a candle by God's grace in England as I trust will never be put out."

John Foxe was to collect all these stories and to publish them later in his Acts and Monuments, better known as the Book of Martyrs. No book did more to fix the Marian tradition and to earn for Mary, who was probably the most merciful of all the Tudors, the title of Bloody Mary and to brand the old faith with the brand of cruelty and terror. But the most important fact was the indelible impression on English minds that Roman Catholicism was the religion of the Inquisition, of the thumb-screw and the stake and that neither its methods nor its purposes were English.

While these things were happening in England, a

company of English Protestant refugees, some 800 of them altogether, at Frankfurt, Strasbourg, and Geneva and elsewhere, who had fled from persecution at home, were maintainting the faith abroad. They all fell definitely under the influence of the Swiss reformers, and their religious thinking was profoundly influenced by the ideas of John Calvin. Most of them were gentlefolk and many of them maintained constant contact with the brethren in England. They drew some support from there and though there is very little evidence to prove that the whole migration was organized in England, certainly the connection between the English reformers who stayed, conformed and rode out the storm and those who fled was a close one. William Cecil, for example, stayed and conformed. His brother-in-law, John Cheke, and his father-in-law, Anthony Cooke, both fled.

After Mary's death the exiles returned. Two of them were to become members of Elizabeth's privy council, two of them her principal secretaries, some ten of them her bishops and two of them her archbishops. Many found places in her House of Commons. In short, they permeated the whole structure of Elizabeth's government and the Elizabethan church. No doubt they were more radical in their religious position when they returned than when they left, more anti-Catholic, more Calvinistic. Some of them had revealed dangerously radical positions in politics, like John Knox and John

Ponet and Christopher Goodman. In their attack upon Mary they had come close to attacking the whole Tudor theory of government. John Knox had some trouble in explaining away his blast of the trumpet against the regiment of women when Elizabeth came to the throne. And he never did explain it away to her satisfaction. Both in their religious and, as it turned out, in their political radicalism, they marked the beginnings of English Puritanism.

III

PURITANISM

Puritanism is an attitude of mind. Beginning as a religious movement it came to embrace a whole social philosophy and a whole political philosophy. It was one of the main springs of democracy, though in itself not necessarily democratic. In the sixteenth century it emphatically was not democratic. Even in puritan New England it was for a long time definitely undemocratic. But the essential elements were always in it, just as they are in the New Testament from which it sprang.

We must ascribe it I think, to some fundamental demand on the part of the human for a close personal relationship with God the Father and a fundamental need for Divine aid in facing the problems of living. The organized church was designed to respond to that need, but as it grew larger and more complex it tended to lose sight of its purpose in preoccupation with the intricacies of its own machinery. Even the Bible itself, the ultimate source of Christian inspiration, tended to become buried in the glosses upon its text, and the simple lessons it taught, in the elaborations of the scholastic philosophy. One really has to begin with the New Testament, for although there were Puritans long before the New Testament became available to the masses of the people, the great forward urge of the

{ 60 }

puritan movement came with the translation of the New Testament into the vernacular.

It has been well said that you can prove anything out of the Bible, and too often it had been used to justify patterns of thought and courses of action which are widely at variance with its essential message. The Puritans were no freer from that fault than the School-men had been. What everyone read in the New Testament was a very simple story of a very primitive church organization. The Puritans found in it an implicit condemnation of all subsequent elaborations of creed, ritual and church organization. Actually of course, when they were faced with the problem of organizing their own church, they discovered that the simple structure of Pauline Christianity was inadequate to meet the needs of a vastly different world. What they thought was simple and easy when they were not in a position of power and responsibility turned out to be something else again when they were. Puritanism in adversity could direct its criticism to what was old and bad and suggest all sorts of fantastic alternatives. But the English Puritans in power never did succeed in establishing a structure, either in religion or politics, which had stability or permanence. Their importance in English history lies rather in what they did as critics and reformers of the old than as creators of the new. Indeed it was as reformers, not as revolutionaries, that they entered the lists and exerted their strength when Elizabeth came to the throne.

Elizabeth herself was no Puritan. She was indeed no religious devotee of any complexion. Essentially she was what the French called a politique, by which I mean that her objectives were primarily political and that she subordinated religious considerations to national ones. She was English first, Protestant afterward. Probably the solution of the religious problem in England which would have come closest to her own ideas was the Henrican Catholicism of her father. Her maternal parentage and the circumstances of her early life, particularly her life in her sister Mary's reign, inevitably committd her to the break from Rome. And she was too sensitive to public opinion to ignore the fact that in the popular mind the Roman connection under Mary had become identified with a hated foreign marriage and a disastrous embroilment in continental wars. But Elizabeth had conformed to Roman Catholicism under Mary and those who knew her best were never too sure that for a substantial consideration in the way of a validating of her title and a firm assurance of her autonomy, she might not return to the fold. To a realist, undisturbed by ideological considerations, there was much to be said for such a course. Her strong neighbors were all Roman Catholic. Her most dangerous competitor, the young Mary Queen of Scots, was Roman Catholic. Probably the majority of her subjects favored the old church as against the new. Her most trusted advisor, William Cecil, himself a politique, though a protestant by choice, had so far made his adjustments to the Roman pattern under Mary, that he was actually one of a committee of three sent to escort Cardinal Pole to England, when he came to give formal Papal blessing to the reestablishment of the old faith.

But Elizabeth was too well aware of the sources of her strength to hesitate. For better or worse she threw in her lot with the reformers and though she never endorsed their position she found their support indispensible. It was not until towards the end of her reign, when Mary Stuart had died at the block and the Spanish Armada had shattered off the Irish coast that she dealt with the Puritans without inhibitions.

Her intention at the very beginning of her reign was to make haste slowly. In her first parliament she introduced a bill establishing the royal supremacy of her church, and it passed with little opposition, though in deference to a rooted prejudice against her sex she declined her father's title of Supreme Head. At the outset she apparently intended to go no further in the reform of that church than her brother Edward had gone in the first year of his reign. But the reformers seem to have forced her hand. It is not a little surprising to discover how strong they were in the House of Commons. The upshot was that they initiated and succeeded in imposing an Act of Uniformity which virtually took over the Edwardian second prayer-book and reestablished the situation as it was in the closing years of her brother's reign. This is not altogether so, Edward's second prayer-book was modified in some particulars, the essential change being the addition of the sentence in the communion service from Edward's first prayer-book which endorsed Cranmer's interpretation of the Real Presence in the sacrament. Elizabeth's prayer-book omitted also the famous Black Rubric. These modifications were in the conservative direction and of course were disagreeable to the Purtians.

The Act of Uniformity which imposed the prayer book was virtually the same as the Edwardian Act, though it did add a fine of one shilling a Sunday to the ecclesiastical censure for those who failed to attend the established church. With these minor modifications, one may fairly say that Elizabeth in her first parliament picked up church reform about where her brother had left it.

The radical reformers did not like it and during the rest of the century they made a valiant effort to change it. Elizabeth was annoyed by their efforts but by no means alarmed. The real menace as she saw it came from the opposite direction. Her religions establishment is ususally described as a via media, – a middle of the road position, – on the right the Roman Catholics on the left the more radical reformers. During the first thirty years of her reign her major problem was to prevent the organization of all the forces of the old faith against her.

On paper they looked much more formidable that any force she could muster in her defense. There was the Most Catholic King of Spain, her brother-in-law, Philip the Second, who on the death of his father a few years before had become master not only of the Spanish dominions on both sides the Atlantic, but also of the Low Countries, the ancient ally of England and the solar-plexus of English export trade.

This factor of the export trade was playing an increasingly important part in the English economy. It was chiefly in one commodity, cloth, and it flowed chiefly through one port, Antwerp. A larger and larger proportion of Englishmen were becoming vitally interested in this trade, at the lower levels as spinners and weavers, at the higher levels as merchants and investors. At the time of Elizabeth's accession the so-called Merchant Adventurers Company, which enjoyed the monopoly of the Antwerp cloth trade, was by far the largest and most influential aggregation of wealth in England. It constituted a powerful pressure group whose objective was to preserve its monopoly and to keep open the channels of trade. At a time when there were no English banks or other domestic sources of short term financing the Merchant Adventurers was the one English group to which the crown could turn for ready cash. Actually, at Elizabeth's succession, the government was almost entirely dependent for short term loans upon the Antwerp money market and one of the major crises of the reign came a few years later when the bankers of Antwerp closed their doors and Elizabeth had to cast frantically about for other sources of credit. One consequence of this situation was that the English government, much against its will, found itself increasingly dependent upon domestic capital and increasingly subservient to it. The cloth trade, the money market, the Low Countries, Spain, – they were all tied together. Of course Philip of Spain had a strong interest in maintaining the lucrative commercial connections between England and his newly acquired Low Countries, though he was temperamentally much less responsive to such considerations than Elizabeth was. And he was of course a newcomer in the Low Countries with none of the inherited traditions of an alliance which dated back at least two hundred years. Nevertheless on both sides economic interests cut sharply across religious ideologies.

Certainly Philip of Spain was the most redoubtable of all the European monarchs. His marriage alliance with Elizabeth's sister, Mary, had symbolized the triumph of a policy designed to unite the forces of England and Spain against France. In principle he was still committed to that alliance, so far committed that he had proposed marriage to Elizabeth almost at the edge of Mary's grave. He may have thought, and indeed had sound reason for thinking, that Elizabeth's initial step toward heresy was tentative and temporary. In orthodox eyes, since Rome did not recognize the legitimacy of her father's marriage with her mother, she was a bastard. But it would not have been difficult to set that matter to rights if she had been so inclined. Elizabeth did not a little to foster this attitude in Philip. Indeed her behavior was so ambiguous that she frightened her own counsellors. And she managed to keep alive in Catholic Europe for ten years the hope that she would return to the old church. They were ten precious years which she turned to very good account in strengthening and solidifying her own position. The whole situation goes far to explain why her attitude towards the radical reformers was so unfriendly and her attitude towards her Roman Catholic subjects so tolerant as in fact it was.

Actually her fears were much greater from France than from Spain. France was after all the traditional enemy as Spain was the traditional friend. And France was more than France; it was, or seemed to be, Scotland as well. The young queen of Scotland, Mary Stuart, was already the wifre of the heir apparent to the French throne and within a year of Elizabeth's succession had become queen of France. Mary was an orthodox Catholic and the heir presumptive to the English throne. On the grounds that Elizabeth was a bastard, Mary was rightful queen of England. She had indeed already adopted that title, had already quartered the English leopards with the French lilies upon her coat of arms.

Here was a combination which might well give Elizabeth pause. There could be very little doubt that the
French did not lack the will to challenge her title. Her
problem was to keep them otherwise engaged. There
was no doubt either that Philip, if he followed the
traditional policy of his house, would resist with all his
force the absorbtion of England by France. The opposing dynastic and national interests of Spain and
France constituted Elizabeth's major safeguard and she
exploited it for all that it was worth. But she never
could be quite sure that dynastic and national interests
would outweigh the interests of the old faith. She
thought they would and she turned out to be right.
But had she been wrong the chances of her survival
under the protestant banner would have been negligible.
Nowhere out of England except in Switzerland and
parts of Germany could the protestants muster any
fighting strength and what they could muster was but a
handful in comparison with the strength which might
have been mustered to destroy them.

It is a significant commentary on the force of religious
zeal in European affairs that the zealots on both sides
failed and the politicians on both sides more or less
succeeded. But that is not to say that religion did not
pay an important part. It played an increasingly important part in Elizabeth's foreign policy. More and
more she found it expedient to play upon religious
dissentions elsewhere in order to divert the attention of

potential enemies. Her timely support of the Scottish protestants enabled them to destroy the French influence in the north. Her support of religious wars in France virtually eliminated France from external aggression of any sort. Her support of the Dutch rebels in the Low Countries was a prime factor in breaking the power of Spain. Much against her will she was more or less forced into the position of protestant leadership, in the old world and even in the new. It was a position which she found extremely distasteful. Certainly she never seriously entertained the idea of an effective protestant union. She always subordinated religious considerations to national ones, and she was always prepared to exploit religious forces in the national interest. In her own mind there was no real conflict between ideologies and interests; she was not troubled by ideologies.

At home the Puritans were never a menace to Elizabeth's position. They were indeed her most dependable supporters. When they took issue with her foreign policy it was only because she put too much trust in princes and not enough in God. The wanted her to come out boldly as the champion of the Reformation and to throw all her strength into the support of Protestantism everywhere. But they constituted after all only a small minority of her people. Most Englishmen at her accession probably preferred the old faith, or at least the Henrican version of it. They accepted the Act of Supremacy without protest but they were not at all disposed to accept the Act of Uniformity. They wanted the old service not the new one, the old priest, not one who must qualify by forswearing the Roman connection. Their resistance to the Elizabethan establishment was at the start a passive one; they simply refused to go to the official church. So we hear of them as Recusants, refusers, not as rebels. In the remoter areas they sometimes maintained their old services and sheltered their old priests. So long as they went no further, the enforcement of the laws against them was languid. The offending priests were hunted down and punished when they were caught, but the laity were left largely undisturbed. The fine for non-attendance was too small to cover the cost of collecting it. And the priests, during the first decade of Elizabeth's reign at any rate, were not of the crusading type. Radical reformers would have welcomed a more aggressive policy, but Elizabeth would have none of it. She accomplished her purpose. Though the Marian bishops almost to a man refused to conform and were deprived, the great mass of the clergy accepted the new arrangement. Probably not more than five percent of them refused. Without much doubt the old church steadily lost ground. This was not accomplished by any policy of active persecution. There were no inquisitions, no martyrs, no stakes. Elizabeth, as she herself is said to have remarked, had no wish to open windows into men's souls. So long as they behaved themselves, what they believed was their own affair. Her success was the success of attrition not of compulsion.

But the cause of Roman Catholicism in England was not to go by default, though the first vigorous efforts in its behalf were to come rather through secular than through religious channels. Just at the end of Elizabeth's first decade came The Rising of the North. Like most rebellions against Tudor rule it sprang from many sources of discontent, some political, some economic, some religious. Probably the religious factor was over-emphasized because it was the factor most likely to attract general support both at home and abroad. A very important factor was the discontent of the old nobility, still particularly strong in the North, against the encroachments of government upon their local autonomy and against the new beaurocracy of par-venues. In this respect the rising of 1569 reflected much the same forces as the Pilgimage of Grace against Henry VIII. It was the last stand of the old pattern against the new, in politics as well as in religion.

Another factor was the arrival of Mary Stuart from over the Scottish border, put completely to rout by the Scottish rebels and claiming protection and support from her cousin Elizabeth. It was probably her arrival and her enthusiastic reception by the northern gentry that brought all the other elements of discontent into focus. Her religion, her position as legitmate successor to Elizabeth, her great personal charm, all contributed.

French aid she could pretty certainly count upon. The Spanish policy of supporting Elizabeth against her had been gravely jeopardized not long after her arrival by Elizabeth's seizure of Spanish ships carrying money for the pay of Spanish armies in the Low Countries. A leader, a cause, loyal supportersa nd foreign aid all seemed implicit in the situation. We need not follow the course of the outbreak that ensued or its failure. Before it was over the Pope fortified the resolution of the rebels by excommunicating Elizabeth and absolving her subjects from their allegiance to her. Foreign aid never arrived, but there was plenty of evidence to indicate that it had been sought and more than half promised.

We must consider the whole problem of Elizabeth's subsequent treatment of her Roman Catholic subjects against this background. Theoretically they were, by the Bull of Excommunication, faced with the definite alternatives of loyalty to the Faith or loyalty to the Crown. To be a Roman Catholic in England was on paper at least to be a traitor. Actually this was far from being the case. Elizabeth, wiser than her counsellors, recognized that notwithstanding papal bulls, Englishmen were Englishmen, and despite their undoubted loyalty to their faith they still preferred a heretic English queen before any foreign alternative. When the Spanish Armada was in the Channel, Catholic gentlemen seized their weapons in defense of their country with no less zeal than their protestant fellows. Nevertheless, while

Mary Stuart was still alive, – and she lived a prisoner in England for nearly twenty years, – the gravest danger which Elizabeth had to face was a Catholic uprising in her favor, supported and assisted by Catholic powers on the continent. In that light the increasing severity of her treatment of them is, if not to be justified at least to be explained. And the danger was emphasized by a definite effort, in the fifteen seventies and fifteen eighties, by devoted Jesuit missionaries to strengthen the faith and to rouse the fighting zeal of the English Catholics. There were no burings at the stake for heresy but there were perhaps too many hangings for treason. Men like Father Edmund Campion showed as much devotion to their faith and as much fortitude in dying for it as any of the Marian martyrs. But the taint of treason was there, not in Campion perhaps but in many who worked alongside of him. During the seventies and the eighties Catholic plot after Catholic plot against the queen was discovered in all of which were the same invariables, Mary, the English Catholics and foreign aid. None of them came anywhere near succeeding. Some of them were exaggerated and some of them may even have been invented by Elizabeth's councillors in order to impress upon her the gravity of the danger which surrounded her. In any case the net result was to create in the English mind an attitude towards Roman Catholicism which embraced Jesuit duplicity, foreign conspiracy, the thumb-screw and the stake of the Inquisition and, must repugnant of all, the subjection of England to foreign rule.

The Puritans worked under no such disadvantage. During Elizabeth's reign they never contemplated foreign intervention in their behalf. Later they were to appeal to a Scottish army against their anointed king, but bij that time what had begun as a movement for reform had developed to the very verge of open rebellion. They were all Calvinists by choice. Virtually all of them accepted the articles of the orthodox faith as expressed in the Thirty-nine Articles, though they looked askance at article twenty-eight in which the Real Presence in the Communion of the Lord's Supper was accepted, albeit in a spiritual sense. The Anglican-Puritan controversy never turned on questions of belief. It turned upon vestments, ritual, ceremonial, and in its later phases, increasingly upon church government. With reference to all of these the Puritans' demand was for greater simplicity and the elimination of everything in the service which smacked of what they would have called Popery. In its initial stages the matter of vestments, that is to say of the distinctive clerical garb which marked off the clergy from the laity, was the chief point at issue. But other ritualistic practises, such as the use of the Sign of the Cross in baptism and the ring in marriage were early objects of attack.

The government in dealing with the situation made much of the vestiarian controversy, in order perhaps to emphasize the fact that what the radicals were making such a fuss about were matters indifferent and that in the interest of uniformity a common practice should be adhered to. Men made much of uniformity in the six-teenth century; deviation meant dissent and dissent was the prelude to rebellion. This attitude of mind was characteristic of all parties. Out of power they pleaded for tolerance, in power almost without exception they imposed rigid conformity to the pattern of their choice. In any case the quarrel over vestments – referred to by one enthusiastic Puritan as 'worse than lousy", like that shirt of Nessus "that made Hercules tear his own bowels asunder" – revealed more fundamental issues. The claim for tolerance, put forward by the moderates, developed among the radicals into something like an appeal to a higher law. There were even those in the first decade of Elizabeth's reign who maintained that the queen herself was subject to the law, not only the common law but the Divine law, and that even she could not command what Holy Writ denied. The matter of Popish vestments, if conceded, would open the door to as many other Popish practices as the royal whim decided. This came perilously close to treason. It was not pressed at this juncture though it became one of the fundamental issues later. What it did reveal was a developing consciousness of a higher law to which man's first allegiance was due. It was not until long afterwards that they thought of rebellion. But some of them, like Robert Crowley, even at the start preached passive resistance. Seek ye first the Kingdom of God and His righteousness and if in that search you must disobey the queen, disobey her and meekly accept her punishment. Do not resist, resign. Obedience to constituted authority had been enjoined by Calvin. The right of resistance he denied, the right of refusal he advocated. Go along with the policeman even if you are sure he is wrong.

Another point of attack was the character of the Anglican clergy, their worldliness, their sycophancy, their conformity to the letter of the law, their neglect of their sacred duties. One hears already of dumb dogs and idle bellies. In a few instances there were those who took matters into their own hands, selected their own own ministers, even ordained them, and created their own congregations. The protest against the worldliness of the Anglican clergy led by degrees to a protest against the whole Anglican system of church government, the imposition from above, not the selection from below. It struck at the lower clergy, nominees for the most part of the country gentry, who regarded these lower positions in the church as belonging to their local patronage and made their appointments too often for reasons quite remote from religious ones. Later it was to strike as high as the bishops. What it meant at bottom was an increasing distrust of secular control of religious affairs. The alternatives the Puritans had in mind were

of the presbyterian variety, though not yet in the democratic pattern of later days. Actually early dissent, so far
as it was concerned not with the reform of the whole
Elizabethan establishment but simply with an immediate
satisfaction of immediate needs, tended towards con-
gregationalism. There was enough official latitude to
admit of action by small groups for reformation, as they
put is, "without tarrying for any". Sometimes when the
local gentry were sympathetic their own rights of patronage could be applied to Puritan purposes and their
police powers utilized to protect small religious establishments which deviated far from orthodox patterns.
Sometime congregations of the faithful took matters
into their own hands as our pilgrim fathers did.

The issue between the more radical reformers and
those who supported the Establishment was brought
into sharp focus in a series of sermons preached at the
Temple Church in London in the fifteen eighties. The
protagonists were Walter Travers and Richard Hooker,
– Travers the Calvinist who had already produced in his
Ecclesiastical Dicipline a systematic exposition of the
Puritan idea of church government; Hooker, the
staunch Anglican. Hooker preached in the morning,
Travers in the afternoon. As Thomas Fuller put it "the
pulpit spake pure Canterbury in the morning and
Geneva in the afternoon". Later Richard Hooker was to
embody his views in his *Laws of Ecclesiastical Policy*,
one of the great books of the century and the ablest of

all presentations of the Anglican position. Much of what Hooker wrote was concerned with the details of Puritan criticism, but his main purpose was to show that the claims of the Puritans to disobey the laws of the church was inconsistent with the nature of politic society. Hooker began at the beginning with the origins of the state, which he found to arise out of a demand for some sort of order out of chaos. He had not in mind any specific social contract, any actual delegation of powers by the people to their governors. He had in mind something vaguer, a recognition of government growing out of the need of it. To him the essence of government was the right to demand obedience. Any admission of a right to disobey was the very negation of government. He admitted a higher law above human law, but he insisted that unless the action of government could be proved beyond peradventure to be contrary to God's law, the duty of obedience was beyond question.

Hooker went on to demonstrate that church and state were simply different aspects of the same commonwealth. The church, he might have said, was the state on Sundays. Man, the citizen, was the same fellow as man, the worshipper. To maintain the contrary was to deny the integrity of the commonwealth. Hooker, like all his contemporaries assumed one church and one state. He assigned religious issues to one of two categories. They were either about matters relatively indifferent or they dealt with questions to which there was no certain answer. About matters indifferent, such as vestments, ritual, church government, the state must decide if only in the interests of unity and publi corder. Clearly no Divine pattern had been provided. God had left these details to human contrivance and centuries of Christian experience had evolved what was substantially the Anglican arrangement. As for the unanswerable questions, they were beyond dispute because they were beyond the range of human capacities to answer. It was better, Hooker thought, that erroneous judgements should be accepted than that vain contentions should disrupt the peace about things indifferent or things indeterminable.

This I take to be the essence of Hooker's position, though of course it lacks his sweet reasonableness of expression and the beauty of his prose. It satisfied the Anglicans but to the Puritans it begged the main question. What Hooker held to be matters indifferent the Puritans held to be matters fundamental. And as for the unanswerable questions they believed that they had the answers in the New Testament and in the Calvinistic theology. So Hooker really left the controversy about where he had found it. It remains not far from that point even to this day, though differences in theology are perhaps less important to us than they were to his contemporaries, and all the Christian churches are I think nearer to an agreement on the essentials of the Christian way of life then ever they were.

It is important that they should be, for the cause they are fighting for in a divided world is fundamentally the Christian cause, which I take to be the freedom of the individual soul to realise the unlimited potentialities for righteousness with which his Creator has endowed him.

Puritanism achieved its plenitude of power in England not so much because of its religious ideas as because of its friends in high places. What we call the Puritan Revolution, which eventuated in the execution of the king and the establishment of a republic was achieved by a combination of forces, the House of Commons, the bar and the Puritans. It was later to appear, when the Commons and the bar turned against the Puritan that he did not have anything like a strong enough following to maintain himself in power. If we describe the first half of the seventeenth century as the period of the triumphant rise of Puritanism we must describe the second half of the century as the period of its decline and fall. Indeed it fell much more rapidly than it had risen. This was due to a combination of circumstances which need not detain us. It did reveal the fact however that Anglicanism in the long run turned out to be more congenial to the English temper than Puritanism, though certainly Puritan ideas have had a profound effect upon the Anglican church and Puritan moral standards have had as profound an influence upon English patterns of behavior as they have had upon our own. It is an almost unique characteristic of the contemporary English labor movement, as contrasted with labor movements elsewhere in Europe, that its socialist ideas are shot through with a strong evangelical strain. Nevertheless, the Puritanism of the sixteenth century never, execpt for a short period, won the day.

The position of dominance which was achieved was temporary and ephemeral, the first fruits of powerful connections. These connections are evident in the House of Commons, the legal profession and, during a large part of Elizabeth's reign, even in her own privy council. During the earlier part of her reign, they are even evident in her episcopate. In her second decade she even had to sequester her Archbishop of Canterbury for his Puritan leanings. Her privy council contained a strong Puritan group. In the seventies and the eighties Sir Francis Walsingham was its leading figure, though he was too good a politician to attempt much direct pressure. The royal favorite, Robert, Earl of Leicester, if he was without religious convictions himself, undertook to exploit the puritan group in his long running fight for preeminence with William Cecil, Lord Burghley. After Leicester's death, in 1588, Robert, Earl of Essex undertook something like the same role in the struggle for preeminence with Cecil's son, Robert, first Earl of Salisbury. In the case of Leicester and perhaps of Essex the Puritan connection was a marriage of convenience.

The position of the Cecils was more ambiguous.

William Cecil had more or less been reared in the Puritan tradition, but like his mistress he always subordinated religious considerations to national ones. He recognized the strength of the Puritans, he recognized also their fervent loyalty, and probably did what he could to develop in his mistress a more tolerant attitude toward them. But he disliked the political implications of their attack upon the established church and he cordially disliked their increasing disrespect of authority. As he grew older and became more conscious of the alliance between Leicester and the Puritans, he seems to have become more conservative. One of his servants, writing of him a few years after his death, summarized his religious views in one sentence, "In matters of religion," he wrote, "Cecil dissented from the papist and the Puritan, disliking the superstition of the one and the singularity of the other; holding the midway between them, as a mean between two extremities." Singularity, in those days, was used to describe those who differed from the generally accepted, deviated from the normal, – that is to say, the inveterate reformers, the perennial agitators.

More significant is the strength of the Puritans in Parliament, particularly in the House of Commons. It is not easy to explain but it revealed itself in the first of Elizabeth's parliaments and it maintained a running fight against the Establishment throughout the reign. Professor Neale has made a careful analysis of the membership of the Elizabethan House of Commons in his admirable book on the subject. He had found that over half of it was drawn from the country gentry, about fifteen percent of it from royal officials and about ten percent of it from practising lawyers. More than half of it had been to the universities or to the law schools.

The university alumni and the lawyers appear to have been those responsible for the Puritan complexion of the House. Family influence had a good deal to do with the attitude of the country gentry, and some of the most influential of the English families were definitely Puritan. This was particularly true of the Hastings and the Russells, the Knollys and the Mildmays, the Dudleys, their kinsfolk the Sidneys, and even the Walsinghams, who controlled directly or indirectly a large number of seats. The Puritans were never in the majority, but they could always muster a vigorous minority, strong enough and courageous enough to give their position emphatic expression. It was Peter Wentworth, Walsingham's brother-in-law, member for Barnstable, who remarked to the Archbishop of Canterbury himself, when the Archbishop was urging him to accept clerical guidance in a matter of church organization: "No," said Wentworth, "by the faith of God, we will pass nothing before we understand what it is. For that were but to make you popes. Make you popes who list, for we will make you none."

Another of Walsingham's brothers-in-law, Robert Beale, who sat for Dorchester in the Parliament of 1584, was one of the leaders in the fight against the procedure of the ecclesiastical Court of High Commission in dealing with the Puritans. Beale, though not himself a lawyer, spoke for the lawyers, and he set forth the issue which had a great deal to do with aligning the profession on the Puritan side. What Beale protested against was the practice of the ecclesiastical commissioners in compelling those brought before them to give, under oath, testimony against themselves; what was called the *ex-officio* oath. This ran counter to the established tradition of the common law courts. The issue developed from the *ex-officio* oath into a jurisdictional dispute between the ecclesiastical courts and the common law courts. And it developed further into an issue between the common law courts and the prerogative courts in general. Could the sovereign create courts of her own devising and develop a special procedure, inquisitorial in character, which ran counter to the whole English legal tradition? It was not only the Court of High Commission which came in question, it was also Star Chamber, Council of the North and other instruments of the Privy Council which, originating in a need for order, had grown to be instruments of despotism.

In its last phase the controversy became one of the subordination of the law to the crown or the crown to the law. We have here a chain reaction which ultimately reached the fundamental question of the location of sovereignty. When that point had been reached it was the House of Commons that defended the law and ultimately imposed it.

By that time the great Queen was long underground. As long as she lived she never allowed the issue of sovereignty to develop. Elizabeth always kept her unerring finger upon the pulse of the English people. She saw to it that her wisest counsellors sat in the House of Commons, and by a kind of instinctive wisdom she knew when she could apply the curb and when she must give free rein. Probably she realized that the England of her later days was not the England of her youth. Mary Stuart was gone, the Armade destroyed, her neighbors no longer a menace. Her corsairs ranged the seven seas, her merchants were spreading in ever widening circles into the markets of the world. Her soldiers and sailors, no longer on the defensive, were carrying the great fight into the very heart of the enemy country. England was safe, more than safe, – England was triumphant. And this new England no longer hesitated to speak its mind. It had its legitimate channel of expression in the House of Commons and more and more as the reign progressed the Commons had come to regard themselves as the mouthpiece of the nation on questions of public policy. They had not hesitated, early in the reign, to speak out frankly on the question of the Queen's marriage. They did not hesitate, notwithstanding royal commands to the contrary, to insist upon the importance of settling the difficult question of the succession. They criticized freely Elizabeth's ecclesiastical arrangements and her fiscal arrangements, and in the very last parliament of her reign they denounced in unmeasured terms her wholesale creation of monopolies. She scolded them, threatened them, disciplined them, but she never broke with them. And whether she resisted their pressure or whether she yielded to it, the final word was always one of affectionate cooperation. Englishmen might cherish many grievances against her government but they never cherished for long any grievance against herself. One gets the impression always that, behind all the incidental bickerings there was deep and abiding confidence, love and loyalty, to the Queen on the part of her subjects and to her subjects on the part of their Queen. She gave voice to this in almost her last public utterance, "Though God," she said, "has raised me high, yet this I account the glory of my crown, that I have ruled with your loves."

The whole situation changed after her death. The smart little Scotsman, a bookish fellow on his spindle shanks, who succeeded her had none of her practical wisdom. Henry of Navarre describe him as the wisest fool in Christendom. He knew the letter of the English constitution, but he never knew the necessity of adjusting it to the demands of a rapidly changing world. And so the conflict moved on to its inevitable climax, and James's son, Charles the First, ended his futile efforts to cope with the situation on the scaffold.

Time does not serve to develop this part of the story which marks the triumph of all the forces which had gathered around Puritanism. It did not mark the triumph of Puritanism, certainly not of its religious programme.

If there was one abiding principle in the whole religious struggle of the sixteenth century, it was the importance of religious uniformity. The Puritans and the Anglicans were at one upon that point. The "outs" may have argued for toleration while they were out, but they never practised it while they were in. In this particular the Puritans were probably worse than their opponents. In any case, uniformity was never achieved. The ultimate answer was an agreement to disagree. One cannot help feeling that religious toleration came rather as the result of fatigue than of conviction. Perhaps we had better say that it came in religion because religion came to matter less.

As we survey the contemporary world we can hardly maintain that mankind today is more tolerant than his forefathers were. He has simply transferred his intolerance to other matters which now command his devotion. Never in modern history has mankind been more sharply divided than mankind is today. The concentration camps of the Germans and the Russians have made the fires of Smithfield look like a genial housewarming; and even in our own blessed country sentiments are expressed by responsible citizens in high places which indicate that we are not yet safe from the Inquisition and some modern, more horrible equivalents of the thumb-screw and stake.

I hesitate to prescribe a remedy. Perhaps the best place to look for it is in the New Testament. The Puritans, for all their attention to it, missed its essential message. We can only pray that at long last we shall be wiser than they.

Printed in the Netherlands
by Drukkerij Meijer, Wormerveer

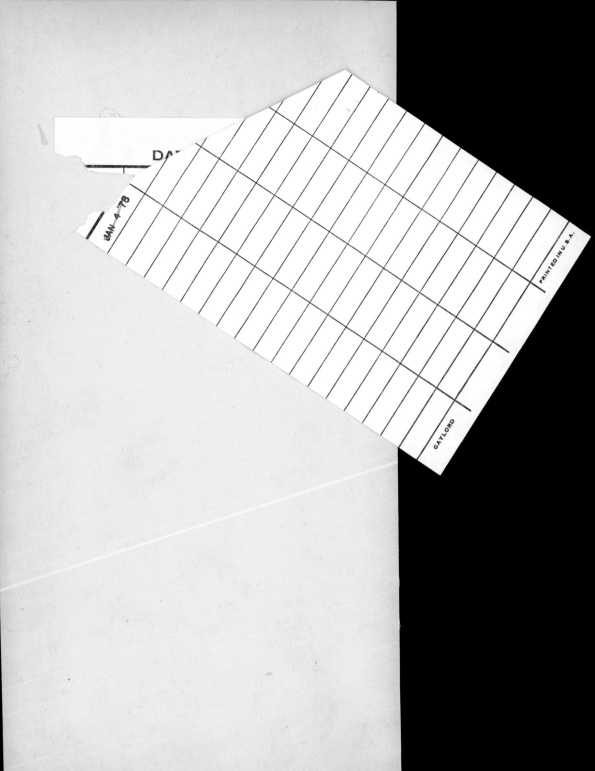